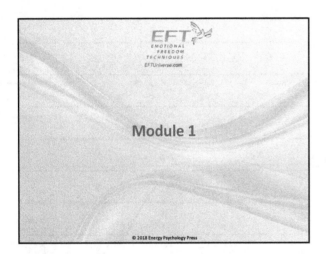

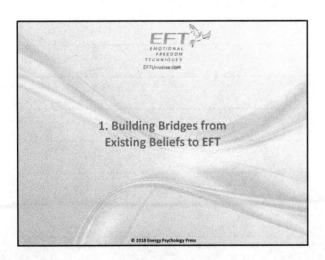

Module 1 Learning Objectives

- **Participants will be able to:**
  1. Name the primary stress hormone.
  2. Characterize the three major parts of the brain.
  3. List two or more of the psychological methods on which EFT is based.

Disclosure of Potential Conflicts of Interest: This workshop is designed to promote evidence-based practice and conform to current professional and ethical standards. While the trainer is receiving financial compensation, he or she is expected to avoid or minimize conflicts of interest, promote objective scientific and educational discourse, provide a fair and balanced assessment of therapeutic options, and present the curriculum free of commercial bias.

- Read *The EFT Manual* (3rd Ed) Chapter 2: The Science Behind EFT

© 2018 Energy Psychology Press

Stress

1.1 Term "Stress" was coined by Hungarian physician Hans Selye in the 1930s to describe symptoms common to many different diseases.

1.2 When we're stressed, it affects our whole body.

© 2018 Energy Psychology Press

1.3 What happens to our nervous system when we are stressed?

1.4 Two halves of autonomic ("automatic") nervous system: sympathetic and parasympathetic.

1.5 Stress activates the sympathetic half. Relaxation activates the parasympathetic half.

1.6 The nerves from the sympathetic and parasympathetic link to every major system.

© 2018 Energy Psychology Press

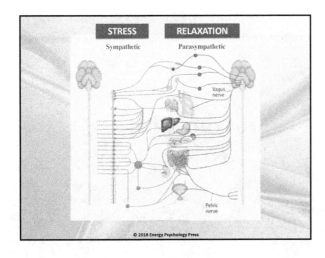

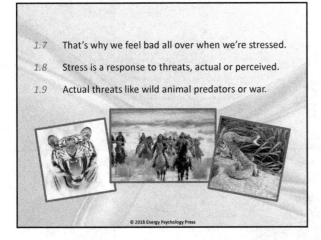

1.7 That's why we feel bad all over when we're stressed.

1.8 Stress is a response to threats, actual or perceived.

1.9 Actual threats like wild animal predators or war.

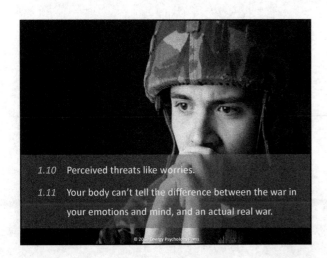

1.10 Perceived threats like worries.

1.11 Your body can't tell the difference between the war in your emotions and mind, and an actual real war.

Sympathetic　　　　**Parasympathetic**

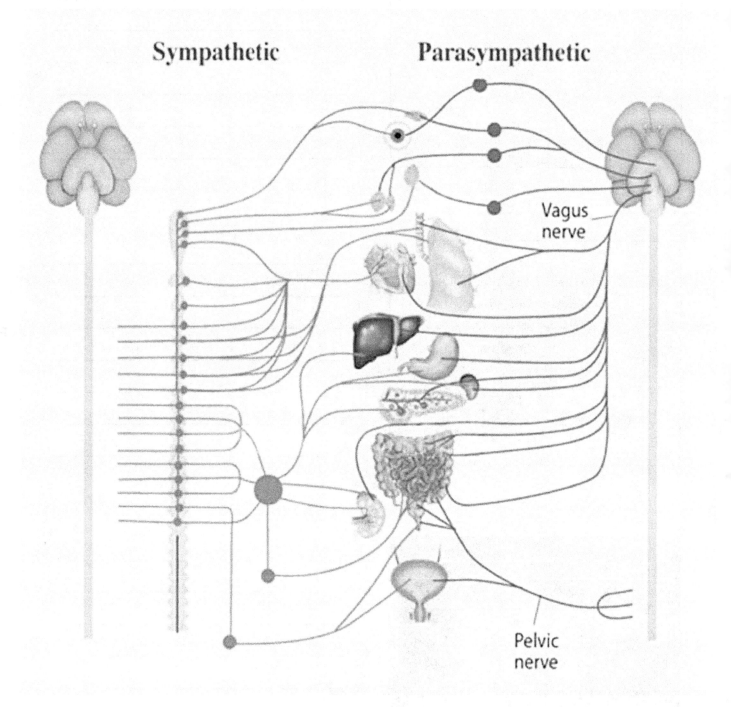

Vagus
nerve

Pelvic
nerve

1.12 Stress

- Stress = Fight or Flight or Freeze Response (FFF)
- Essential to Survival
- Evolutionary Biology
- Foundation of Hierarchy of Needs

Effects of Stress on Endocrine System

1.13 What happens to our hormones, adrenaline, cortisol, and DHEA, when we are stressed?
- Our adrenal glands increase production of adrenaline.
- Our endocrine glands increase production of cortisol (stress hormone).
- They decrease production of dehydroepiandrosterone (DHEA).

1.14 When we're relaxed, we make lots of DHEA (cell repair hormone). We use the same precursors to build both DHEA and cortisol, and our body shunts production between the two depending on how stressed we are.

1.15 The Triune Brain

- Hindbrain: Reptile, lizard. Handles survival needs, instinctual response to threats.
- Midbrain/Limbic: Mammalian; horse, dog. Handles socialization, memory of threats, anticipation.
- Forebrain/Cerebrum: Primates, chimp, human. Handles cognition, executive functions, discrimination.

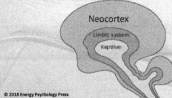

1.16 Effects of Stress on the Brain

- When you're stressed, up to 70% of the blood drains from your frontal lobes into your peripheral muscles. You don't need to be able to perform calculus when you're running from a tiger.

- The problem is that paper tigers in thought, memory, or anticipation trigger the other lobes: worry creates stress.

- Adaptive for archaic societies, not so adaptive for modern humans.

© 2018 Energy Psychology Press

1.17 Interdependent Systems

STRESS		RELAXATION
Sympathetic	*Nervous System*	Parasympathetic
Cortisol	*Hormone*	DHEA
Beta	*Brain Wave*	Alpha
Dopamine	*Neurotransmitter*	Serotonin

© 2018 Energy Psychology Press

1.18 EFT Is a Stress-Reduction Technique

It combines physical stimulation and remembering a traumatic event (exposure).

1.19. EFT uses natural stress-reduction points
- o *Collarbone*
- o *Around eyes*
- o *Chin*

© 2018 Energy Psychology Press

1.19 EFT Is a Stress-Reduction Technique

Acupuncture sends stress-reduction signals to parts of the brain that are activated by fear.

o *Acupuncture is being used by the US Army to treat posttraumatic stress disorder (PTSD) with soldiers post-deployment.*

o *The Veterans Stress Project is a network of practitioners providing free sessions to veterans.*

© 2018 Energy Psychology Press

1.20 EFT Can Be Briefly Explained as:

- A relaxation technique
- A stress-reduction technique
- An emotional version of acupuncture

© 2018 Energy Psychology Press

1.21 EFT Is Part of the Field of Energy Psychology

- There are about 30 methods of Energy Psychology
  - o *EFT is the most widely used.*
  - o *Over 3 million visitors/month to the 5 most popular EFT sites, over 8 million Google searches/month.*
  - o *EFT was adapted from Thought Field Therapy as a simplified version by a Stanford-trained engineer and performance coach.*

© 2018 Energy Psychology Press

1.22 Historically, the Elements of EFT Came from:

Psychology
- *Holistic Psychology* (Wundt: Body and Mind Interact, Leipzig, 1870s)
- *Conditioning* (Pavlov: Dogs, Russia, 1920s)
- *Counterconditioning* (Wolpe: SUD, US, 1950s)
- *Behavior Therapy* (Skinner: Small Parts of Each Behavior, US, 1930s)
- *Cognitive Therapy* (Ellis, Beck: Cognitions Affect Stress, US, 1960s)
- *Human Potential & Client-Centered Therapy Movements* (Maslow, Rogers: Self-actualization, 1960s)
- *(Continued)*

© 2018 Energy Psychology Press

1.22 Historically (Continued)

- *Exposure Therapy*

(Edna Foa: Prolonged Focus on Problem, 1980s)

- *Thought Field Therapy*

(Callahan: Acupoints Affect Psychological Symptoms, 1970s)

© 2018 Energy Psychology Press

1.23 Physics

- The awareness that energy affects matter ($E = mc^2$).
- Discovery of the electromagnetic field of the human heart, 1903, Willem Einthoven, Nobel Prize for Medicine, 1924.
- The human heart has the strongest electromagnetic field of all human organs.

The Heart's Electromagnetic Energy Field

© 2018 Energy Psychology Press

1.23 Physics (Continued)

- Hans Berger, EEG, discovered field of the brain, 1924.
- Today's MRIs, EEGs, EKGs, EMGs, PEMS, TENS machines all use fields.

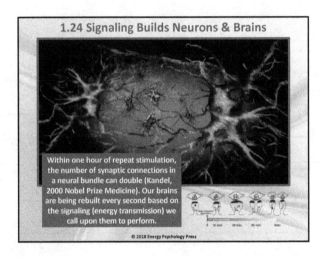

Hans Berger's First EEG Recording, 1924

- String Theory: What we perceive as matter may actually be strings of energy vibrating at different frequencies.

© 2018 Energy Psychology Press

1.24 Signaling Builds Neurons & Brains

Within one hour of repeat stimulation, the number of synaptic connections in a neural bundle can double (Kandel, 2000 Nobel Prize Medicine). Our brains are being rebuilt every second based on the signaling (energy transmission) we call upon them to perform.

© 2018 Energy Psychology Press

1.24.1 Large vs. Small Neural Bundles

- Under stress, signals flow through larger pathways.

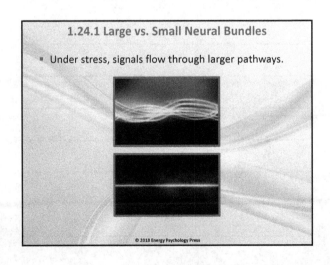

© 2018 Energy Psychology Press

1.25 EFT's "Discovery Statement"

- "The cause of all negative emotion is a disruption in the body's energy system."

- This was an early attempt to explain EFT's rapid effects. It dates from the period before scientific discoveries in epigenetics, neural plasticity, evolutionary biology, and psychoneuroimmunology provided insights into the many causes of negative emotion.

© 2018 Energy Psychology Press

1.26 The Metaphor of Interference

- Similar to interference with a signal, like mountains interfering with cell reception.

- Acupuncture teaches that energy flows in meridians, and that physical or emotional problems result if the energy is blocked.

- The purpose of energy psychology methods is to remove the blockages.

© 2018 Energy Psychology Press

1.27 Building Bridges for Understanding EFT

So now we've built bridges to:
- o Evolutionary Biology
- o Cognitive Neuroscience
- o Electromagnetic Fields in Medicine
- o Energy Fields in Acupuncture
- o Modern Psychological History
- o Experimental Psychology
- o The Stress Response
- o Neural Plasticity, Triune Brain, Signal Transmission

Tutorial #13: "Building Bridges to Believability"

© 2018 Energy Psychology Press

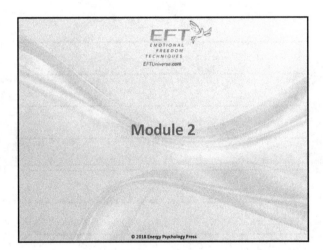

Module 2 Learning Objectives

- **Participants will be able to:**

  1. Demonstrate EFT's core technique, the "Basic Recipe."

  2. Describe the meaning of "secondary gain."

  3. Name at least one optional tapping acupoint.

  4. State what the acronym "SUD" stands for.

- Read *The EFT Manual* (3rd Ed) Chapter 3: The Basic Recipe, and Appendix A: The Full Basic Recipe

© 2018 Energy Psychology Press

How to Calm Stress & Be Happy

- *2.1.* The central human problem, from Plato to the Buddha to today, is how to be happy and escape the cycle of suffering.

- *2.2.* EFT is a simple, mechanical method of stress relief. It does not require belief.

- Emotional WD-40

© 2018 Energy Psychology Press

2.3 EFT's Full Basic Recipe

1. State the Problem
2. Subjective Units of Distress (SUD) #1
3. The "Setup Statement" 2 parts
4. Reminder Phrase
5. The 4 Steps of EFT's Full Basic Recipe
   - *Step 1*: Setup Statement
   - *Step 2*: Sequence of tapping (w/ reminder statements)
   - *Step 3*: 9 Gamut
   - *Step 4*: Sequence of tapping (w/ reminder statements)
6. SUD #2

© 2018 Energy Psychology Press

EFT's Full Basic Recipe (Continued)

2.4. Problem

- Aim it at any emotional or physical problem
  - Customize with appropriate Setup affirmation and Reminder Phrase
- Be specific when possible
  - Aim EFT at the specific emotional events in your life that might underlie the problem. Spray the lubricating oil on the squeaky hinge, not the whole door.
- (Continued)

© 2018 Energy Psychology Press

EFT's Full Basic Recipe (Continued)

- Test
  - ○ *Check progress by checking in with yourself or client*
- Subjective Units of Distress (SUD)
  - ○ *Intensity scale of 0 to 10*

10
9
8
7
6
5
4
3
2
1
0

© 2018 Energy Psychology Press

EFT's Full Basic Recipe (Continued)

2.5. **The "Setup Statement" is an elegant 3-part formula, bracketing the problem with exposure and self-acceptance:**

- Acknowledgment (stated before the problem):
  - ○ *"Even though…"*
- The problem (exposure)
  - ○ *"…I have this problem…"*
- Cognitive acceptance (stated after the problem):
  - ○ *"…I deeply and completely accept myself"*

Exposure		Cognitive Framing
Even though	The Problem	I deeply and completely accept myself

© 2018 Energy Psychology Press

EFT's Full Basic Recipe (Continued)

2.6. Repeat these 3 parts in conjunction with one another, 3 times while rubbing the Sore Spot (on the chest, 2 in./5 cm. below the collarbone on either side) or tapping the Side of Hand point (the fleshy side of the hand below the pinkie on either hand).

2.7. Tap on the other points while repeating the Reminder Phrase.

© 2018 Energy Psychology Press

EFT's Full Basic Recipe (Continued)

2.8. **Reminder Phrase**

▪ Choose a phrase that triggers the maximum emotional response while you are tapping.

▪ You do not need to repeat the full Setup Statement, simply use the Reminder Phrase, a shortened version or selection of words from the Setup Statement that remind you of the problem.

_____
_____
_____
_____
_____
_____
_____

2.9 Tapping Points

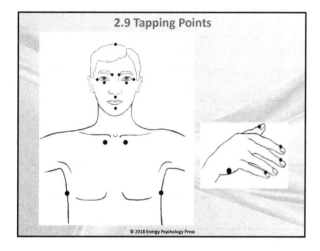

_____
_____
_____
_____
_____
_____

2.10 The 9 Gamut

Perform 9 steps while tapping "Gamut point" (back of hand between bones anchoring last 2 fingers) continuously.

1. *Eyes closed.*
2. *Eyes open.*
3. *Eyes down hard right while holding the head steady.*
4. *Eyes down hard left while holding the head steady.*
5. *Roll eyes in a circle. Head steady, eyes in big slow circle at the extreme edge of peripheral vision.*
6. *Roll eyes in a circle in the reverse direction.*
7. *Hum 2 seconds of any song.*
8. *Count rapidly from 1 to 5.*
9. *Hum 2 seconds of a song again.*

_____
_____
_____
_____
_____
_____

2.11 EFT's Shortcut: The Basic Recipe

- **Step 1:** Setup Statement (while tapping Karate Chop point)

- **Step 2:** Sequence of tapping other points (with Reminder Phrases)

- You leave out the 9 Gamut, the second Sequence, and the hand points.

© 2018 Energy Psychology Press

Exercise 1

Practice EFT using the Shortcut and Full Basic Recipe. Think of an upsetting scene. It could be from a news story, social media post, movie, book or documentary.

Write down:

- Your first SUD score
- Where in your body you feel intensity
- The name of your issue. Pick a recent minor annoyance with a SUD of 5 or less
- After EFT, your second SUD score

© 2018 Energy Psychology Press

Exercise 1

Scene from a Disturbing Show
- Tap on a scene from a disturbing show
  - Run the clip in your mind
  - Evaluate the intensity you are having using SUD
  - Take the edge off with EFT
  - Verbally narrate the scene
  - Stop at any upset and repeat EFT

© 2018 Energy Psychology Press

2.12 Subsequent Round Adjustments

Has your SUD score not come down much?
Do EFT on the remaining intensity.

Setup Statement:
"Even though I still have some of this _____ problem"

Reminder Phrase: *"This remaining _____ problem."*

Persist.

2.13 Psychological Reversal

Psychological Reversal was first articulated by Dr. Callahan in the Thought Field Therapy tapping method.

- His metaphor for the idea was:
  - *"Beginning a tapping session without first setting up the polarity of the body is like putting batteries into a flashlight backwards – with the polarity switched."*

- The light will not shine

2.13 Psychological Reversal (Continued)

- Human energy circuits also need proper polarity.

- This led to the idea that, in a psychologically reversed client, the body's energy flows backwards.

- In acupuncture, blockages in meridians are believed to prevent the flow of life energy and are resolved by needling.

2.13 Psychological Reversal (Continued)

- *2.13.1* Psychological reversal is a state or condition that blocks natural healing and prevents otherwise effective treatments from working.

- *2.13.2* The psychologically reversed state is usually accompanied by negative attitudes and self-sabotaging behavior.

- *2.13.3* In everyday life, psychological reversal is often recognized as the "psychological block" that prevents us from accomplishing certain tasks with ease.

2.13 Psychological Reversal (Continued)

- We tap the Karate Chop point or rub the Sore Spot to clear energy blockages.

  o *These blockages can negate EFT's effects.*
  o *They can occur repeatedly during a session.*
  o *That's why we correct for psychological reversal at the start of every round of tapping.*

2.14 Secondary Gain: the Upside of the Downside

- Addressing and removing the negatives will also have positive effects.

  o *However, if the negatives have an upside, they will be harder to clear. The negatives may seem more attractive than healing.*

- Safety issues: where the problem keeps you safe

  o *For example, an overweight woman whose weight protects her from unwanted attention.*

- Security issues: where the problem provides security

  o *Such as a man's primary source of income being a disability check for a bad neck.*

2.15 Additional Tapping Points

- Wrist
  - o *Sensitive spot two thumb-widths from wrist crease.*
- Ankle
  - o *Find outside of ankle bone, go up 4" (not indicated for first and last month of pregnancy).*
- Side of Thigh
  - o *Spot where the palms touch the outer thighs while standing. Used in EMDR.*

© 2018 Energy Psychology Press

2.16 Why EFT Doesn't Focus on the Positive First

- Addressing and removing the negatives will also have positive effects.
- Going for the positives first is like dressing a wound without cleaning that wound – it is much more likely to turn into a worse problem, like an infection.
- Healing the negatives is natural and must come before tapping for the positive.

The curious paradox is that when I accept myself just as I am, then I can change.
-Carl Rogers (1961, p. 17)

© 2018 Energy Psychology Press

Confidentiality

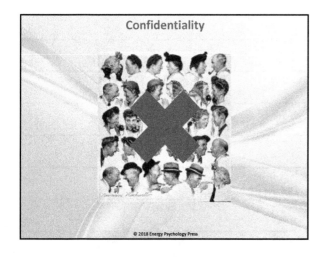

© 2018 Energy Psychology Press

TRAINER INSIGHTS

Question & Answer

Lunch Break

© 2018 Energy Psychology Press

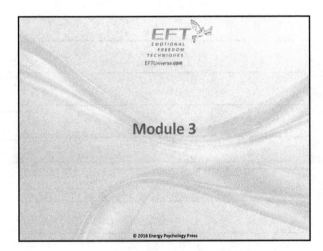

Module 3

© 2018 Energy Psychology Press

Module 3 Learning Objectives

- **Participants will be able to:**

  1. Identify at least two different aspects of an event.

  2. Name one method of testing the results of EFT.

  3. Identify one physiological sign of relaxation.

- Read *The EFT Manual* (3rd Ed) Chapter 3: The Basic Recipe

© 2018 Energy Psychology Press

3.1 The Importance of Being Specific

- Imagine doing a Google search for a term. If you search for *"annoyance"* you get millions of hits. If you search for *"annoyed by Jim saying 'I don't care' on Saturday night,"* you get just one.
  - *Since the second search is more specific, it is more likely to activate the neural circuits associated with the disturbing memory so that they can be counterconditioned.*
- Tutorial #4: *"The Importance of Being Specific"*

© 2018 Energy Psychology Press

3.2 The Importance of Being Specific (Continued)

- EFT works the same way – your body will heal with EFT much better if you are specific as to where the problem is.
  - *Ask simple questions to narrow down the client's distress to a disturbing specific event.*
  - *Memories are laid down as single events, not overall diagnoses like "anxiety".*
  - *To access a memory with EFT, you must focus on the single event and not the diagnosis.*
  - *Use exact words – write them down, if necessary.*
  - *Tap along with client, use exact words, creates security.*

© 2018 Energy Psychology Press

Aspects (Parts of an Event)

3.3. Aspects are parts of a problem or event. Do EFT for a single aspect of the problem until SUD is low, then move to the next part.

- Tutorial #5: *"Aspects"*

© 2018 Energy Psychology Press

Aspects

3.4. Example of aspects of a car crash:

- *Scent of burning rubber and blood (smell—olfactory aspect)*
- *Image of the other car about to hit (sight—visual aspect)*
- *Crash of breaking glass (sound—auditory aspect)*
- *Sensation of hands pulling me out (touch—kinesthetic aspect)*
- *Taste of blood in my mouth (taste—gustatory aspect)*
- *Heavy sensation in gut when I think about it (bodily feeling—somatic aspect)*
- *Guilt about totaling Dad's car (emotion—emotional aspect)*

© 2018 Energy Psychology Press

Aspects

3.5. Aspects often encode information from each sensory channel. Notice how the car crash includes touch, smell, sight, sound, taste. Asking client about these may uncover new aspects. May also include emotions, images, cognitions, beliefs, verbal cues, and physical feelings.

© 2018 Energy Psychology Press

Exercise 2: Aspects

Form groups of 3: Coach, Client, and Observer.

Play the Aspect Game to see how many aspects you can find.

- ***Step 1:*** *Client and coach: Tap continuously, don't stop tapping from the start of the exercise until the end.*
- ***Step 2:*** *Client: Talk about a problem while tapping.*
- ***Step 3:*** *Client: Skip freely from memory to memory and aspect to aspect as they arise. Free association.*

(Continued)

© 2018 Energy Psychology Press

The Aspects Game
How many aspects can your group find?

#	Aspect	#	Aspect	#	Aspect
1		26		51	
2		27		52	
3		28		53	
4		29		54	
5		30		55	
6		31		56	
7		32		57	
8		33		58	
9		34		59	
10		35		60	
11		36		61	
12		37		62	
13		38		63	
14		39		64	
15		40		65	
16		41		66	
17		42		67	
18		43		68	
19		44		69	
20		45		70	
21		46		71	
22		47		72	
23		48		73	
24		49		74	
25		50		75	

Exercise 2: Aspects (Continued)

o **Step 4:** *Coach: Tap along with client. If client gets stuck, ask about each of the 5 senses : "What did you see, hear, touch, taste, smell?". If client keeps talking, let them talk.*

o **Step 5:** *Client and coach: Don't worry about getting SUD, Reminder Phrase, or anything except tapping through aspects.*

o **Step 6:** *Observer: Write down the name of each aspect on the Session Notes form. Count the total.*

© 2018 Energy Psychology Press

3.6 Try It on Everything

- EFT works for a wide variety of problems – and it never hurts to try!
- You can use EFT on physical sensations, emotions, symptoms, events, and beliefs.
- Tapping has shown surprisingly positive results in many areas including pain, performance anxiety, depression, traumatic stress, negative beliefs, sports performance, relationship quality, fear, burnout, and autoimmune diseases.
- The reason for this is that stress is a component of all of these.
- Tutorial #3: *"Try it on Everything!"*

© 2018 Energy Psychology Press

Testing

3.7. Test continuously for SUD intensity on the scale from 0 to 10.

3.8. Learn
  o *When to try for 0*
  o *When to accept less than 0*

© 2018 Energy Psychology Press

Testing

3.9. Observe physiological signs of release.

- *Shoulders slacken, breathing calms, heartbeat goes down, facial flushing, sweating*

© 2018 Energy Psychology Press

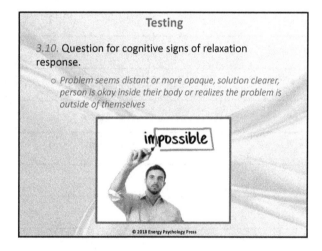

Testing

3.10. Question for cognitive signs of relaxation response.

- *Problem seems distant or more opaque, solution clearer, person is okay inside their body or realizes the problem is outside of themselves*

impossible

© 2018 Energy Psychology Press

EFT
EMOTIONAL
FREEDOM
TECHNIQUES
EFTUniverse.com

TRAINER INSIGHTS

Question & Answer

© 2018 Energy Psychology Press

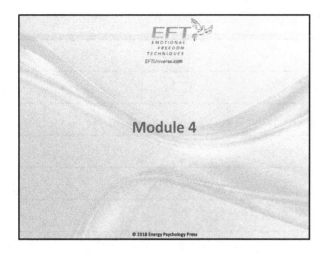

Module 4

© 2018 Energy Psychology Press

Module 4 Learning Objectives

- **Participants will be able to:**
  1. Define "the generalization effect."
  2. Define what EFT means by the term "Borrowing Benefits" in group sessions.

- Read *The EFT Manual* (3rd Ed) Chapter 3: The Basic Recipe

© 2018 Energy Psychology Press

Using EFT in Groups

© 2018 Energy Psychology Press

4.1 Borrowing Benefits

- While witnessing a session, you tap along with client.
- Focus on your own issues. Get SUD levels before and after.
- This usually results in a drop in SUD levels in witness as well as client.
- Applies to: Coach-client sessions. Videos. Live group sessions. Group teleclasses. Webinars.
- Use Borrowing Benefits for each demonstration in workshops.

4.2 Healthcare Workers Study

Large study of Borrowing Benefits published in the peer-reviewed journal *Integrative Medicine*.

One-day EFT workshop with 216 participants at five professional conferences Borrowing Benefits in groups. Doctors, psychotherapists, nurses, chiropractors, alternative medicine practitioners. Measured:

- Psychological conditions such as anxiety (ANX) and depression (DEP)
- Breadth of psychological symptoms (GSI)
- Depth of psychological symptoms (PST)
- Pain
- Cravings
- The intensity of a single intense emotional memory (Emo)

Church, D., & Brooks, A. J. (2010). The effect of a brief EFT (Emotional Freedom Techniques) self-intervention on anxiety, depression, pain and cravings in healthcare workers. *Integrative Medicine: A Clinician's Journal*, 9(4), 40–44.

4.3 EFT Reduced Psychological Symptoms

The overall severity of psychological symptoms severity dropped by 45%. Significant reductions in Anxiety (Anx), Depression (Dep), and other conditions (all $p < 0.001$).

4.4 EFT Reduced Physical Symptoms

Pain dropped by 68%, the intensity of a traumatic memory by 83%, and cravings by 83% (all $p < 0.001$). Participants maintained their gains on follow-up. Later replicated (Palmer-Hoffman & Brooks, 2011).

© 2018 Energy Psychology Press

4.5 The Generalization Effect

4.5.1. Sometimes, knocking out one problem can be like knocking down a table.

- *You can hack away at the surface... but if you take out one of the legs, the whole table can go down.*
- *The whole problem, similarly, can disappear if the right legs are taken out from under it.*

© 2018 Energy Psychology Press

4.6 Handling Excessive Intensity

EFT works well as a tool for handling excessive intensity (uncontrollable crying, emotional flooding, inability to speak).

Just keep tapping. OK to talk, as long as you're tapping too.

© 2018 Energy Psychology Press

4.7 Disproportionate Responses

- When the emotional output you produce is disproportionate to the emotional input signal.

- To stimuli such as:
  - ○ *Traffic signals*
  - ○ *Bad drivers*
  - ○ *Work meetings*
  - ○ *Political parties*

© 2018 Energy Psychology Press

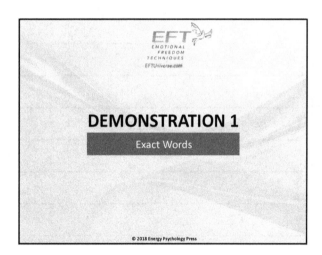

DEMONSTRATION 1
Exact Words

© 2018 Energy Psychology Press

Exercise 3: Exact Words

Split into Triads (Coach, Client, and Observer)

- ○ **Client:** *Talk about what is seen and felt during a typical specific incident to which you have a disproportionate response. Provide no history or explanation.*

- ○ **Coach:** *Repeat exact words back, while tapping. Don't interpret, explain, reframe, or try and be helpful.*

- ○ **Observer:** *Interrupt Coach if Coach does anything other than feed back exact words.*

© 2018 Energy Psychology Press

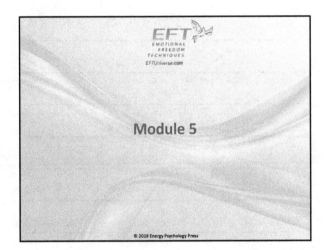

Module 5 Learning Objectives

▪ **Participants will be able to:**

1. Name at least two possible signs of a cognitive shift.

2. Identify at least two characteristics of a traumatizing event.

▪ Read *The EFT Manual* (3rd Ed) Chapter 6: The Gentle Techniques (pages 175-190)

© 2018 Energy Psychology Press

5. Cognitive Belief Shifts

5.1. EFT produces the ability to integrate memory with life.

5.2. When we are comfortable with an event, there is no emotional charge.

  o *A well-processed trauma, however, will have no emotional charge (Example: a dog chasing a cat, afterwards cat grooms to self-soothe).*

© 2018 Energy Psychology Press

---

5. Cognitive Belief Shifts (Continued)

5.3. Tapping on an unprocessed trauma can bring a cognitive shift towards feelings of being at peace, of having moved on, of being safe. The client may now imagine themselves as a spectator of the traumatizing event, not a participant. A memory that was vivid may become fuzzy, or the reverse – a fuzzy memory may come into sharp focus. A client may also shift from a victim perspective to feeling compassion towards the perpetrator.

5.4. Cognitive shifts often happen in the background.

© 2018 Energy Psychology Press

5.5 The Characteristics of Traumatizing Events

- Perceived threats to physical survival

- Event overwhelms coping capacity, producing a sense of powerlessness

- Feeling of isolation, aloneness

- Feeling that expectations have been violated

© 2018 Energy Psychology Press

0

5.6 The Trauma Capsule

- The brain stops remembering a moment before the specific event begins and resumes after it ends, in order to protect us from the traumatic event.

Trauma Capsule

SUD

10
8
6
4
2
0

Memory

© 2018 Energy Psychology Press

5.7 Unprocessed Trauma

- Can't integrate the trauma into experiences

- Trauma is frozen in time, experienced in the present tense

- Sensory aspects such as touch, hearing, sensations and emotions are all inside the capsule

- To our distant ancestors, the ability to remember traumatic cues ensured their survival. The emotional midbrain contains structures to hardwire them. The *hippocampus* (memory and emotional learning) signals the *amygdala* (the alarm response) when a threat is perceived.

© 2018 Energy Psychology Press

5.8 How Trauma Is Reinforced in the Brain

Trauma is reinforced through:

o *Conditioned feedback loops*

o *Neurogenesis*

© 2018 Energy Psychology Press

5.9 Symptoms of Trauma (DSM)

- Intrusive thoughts
- Nightmares
- Flashbacks
- Dissociation
- Dysfunctional Cognitive Associations
- Hypervigilance
- Avoidance

5.10 The Role of Insight and Therapy

- Don't you need insight? Doesn't everyone need insight?
- Aren't explanations based on childhood and subconscious experiences essential?

FFT
EMOTIONAL
FREEDOM
TECHNIQUES
EFTUniverse.com

TRAINER INSIGHTS SLIDE
Question & Answer

EFT
EMOTIONAL
FREEDOM
TECHNIQUES
EFTUniverse.com

Module 6

© 2018 Energy Psychology Press

Module 6 Learning Objectives

▪ **Participants will be able to:**

1. Describe at least three of the steps of EFT's "Movie Technique."

2. Identify one behavioral characteristic of emotional flooding.

▪ Read *The EFT Manual* (3rd Ed) Chapter 3: The Basic Recipe

© 2018 Energy Psychology Press

6.1 Taking the Edge off Excessive Intensity

Excessive emotional intensity
▪ Crying uncontrollably, unable to speak
▪ Can trigger coach
▪ Can trigger client further: emotional flooding

Exception to the rule of being specific:
▪ Here we can use global statements

© 2018 Energy Psychology Press

6.2 Sneaking Away

- At the end of a session, the emotional work is often incomplete.
- Sneaking Away is an elegant way to wrap up the session.
- Provides temporary closure to client.
- Tap while using phrases such as:
  o *"Even though we haven't dealt with all of this"*
  o *"Even though I have to come back next week"*
  o *"Even though I think I'll never get over this"*
  o *"We'll put this into a box..."*
- At the end of a session, return the client's attention to the here and now. Examples: Have the client look around the room. Ask about the time and the weather.

© 2018 Energy Psychology Press

6.3 "Silent Movie" and "Tell the Story" Techniques

- Identify a single brief triggering scene. Give it a title. Tap for the title alone until SUD score is 2 or less.
- Start from a neutral point.
- Whenever intensity crescendos, tap until it is at 3 or less.
- Rewind and start again from a neutral point.
- Continue until next crescendo in intensity, then repeat.
- When you can get through the whole movie without increasing in intensity, test by re-telling.

© 2018 Energy Psychology Press

6.4 Clearing the Trauma Capsule

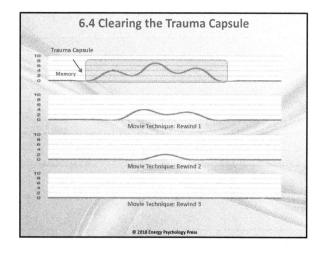

© 2018 Energy Psychology Press

6.5 The Silent Movie Technique

Preparing for Demo & Exercise

- Pick a single incident that happened in adulthood.
- How long is the movie?
- What is the title?

Tutorial #6: *"The 'Tell The Story' Technique"*

Tutorial #7: *"The Movie Technique"*

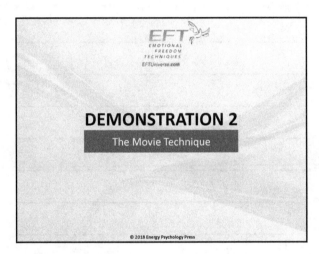

EFT
EMOTIONAL
FREEDOM
TECHNIQUES
EFTUniverse.com

DEMONSTRATION 2
The Movie Technique

Exercise 4: The Silent Movie Technique

- Pick a single incident that happened in adulthood.
- How long is the movie?
- What is the title? When you're in the Coach role, work the title into a Setup Statement and do the Movie Technique with your client.
- Practice doing the 9 Gamut on at least one aspect of the movie. Use BIG circles at the very edge of your client's peripheral vision.
- Sneak away if the client's SUD score is still high at the end of the session.

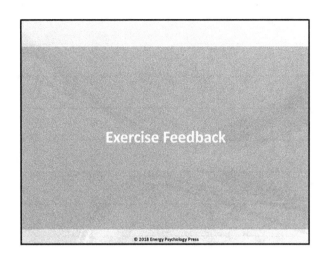

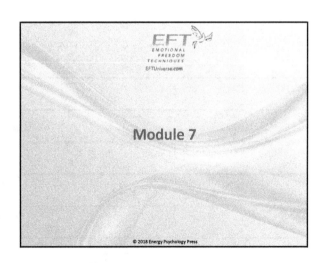

Module 7 Learning Objectives

▪ **Participants will be able to:**

1. List at least two questions to ask a client to identify emotional correlates of physical pain.

2. Name one method of validating different parts of the self.

▪ Read *The EFT Manual* (3rd Ed) Chapter 8: Special Populations

7.1 EFT for Physical Symptoms

▪ Pain

▪ Energy toxins and allergens

▪ Find triggers to basic questions of: when, where, how, with who, all thoughts, feelings

▪ What is the first question to ask? "Have you seen a doctor?"

▪ Work on the emotional aspects with EFT and with conventional and alternative medicine on medical conditions

7.2 Be Curious About Symptoms

▪ Are they diffused? Sharp? Hot? Cold? What is the composition? Color? Movement? Vibration?

▪ Ask where and when the pain symptom is triggered.

▪ Are there situations in which it is not triggered?

7.3 Tapping for Aspects of Pain

▪ Tap for:
  ○ *The pain itself*
  ○ *Experiences occurring in life when the pain started*
  ○ *Emotions associated with that part of the body*

▪ The protective function of pain
▪ Is there secondary gain associated with the pain?
▪ Give the pain a voice, have a dialog with it

Module 8

© 2018 Energy Psychology Press

Module 8 Learning Objectives

▪ **Participants will be able to:**

1. Cite examples of cognitive statements to use with a client presenting with the problem of self-acceptance.

2. Distinguish between cravings and addiction.

▪ Read *The EFT Manual* (3rd Ed) Chapter 5: Common Questions, Comments, and Problems

© 2018 Energy Psychology Press

---

8. When EFT Doesn't Work

8.1. Are you being too global? Also try:

8.2. Other possibilities:

- ○ *You're working on an adult memory when the problem originated in childhood. Go as early as possible.*
- ○ *Look for a larger or deeper emotional issue.*
- ○ *Find additional aspects of the triggering event.*
- ○ *Describe minute details of the triggering event.*
- ○ *Fish for related events.*
- ○ *Raise your voice, exaggerate, generalize, swear, have a pity party.*
- ○ *Refer to a practitioner specializing in that issue.*

© 2018 Energy Psychology Press

8. When EFT Doesn't Work (Continued)

8.3. Mechanical Techniques:
- *Do the 9 Gamut repeatedly and slowly, especially covering visual quadrants the client is skipping.*
- *Emphasize tapping the Karate Chop point because the client might have persistent psychological reversal.*
- *Try the Sore Spot instead of the Karate Chop point.*
- *Try psychological reversal corrections from Energy Medicine like Cook's Hook Up or the Cross Crawl.*
- *Drink water.*
- *Test for energy toxins.*

Tutorial #17: *"Finding Core Issues"*

8.4 When Self-Acceptance Is the Problem

Try *"accept myself"* instead of *"love myself"*
- Alternate Setup phrases:
  - *I'm doing my best*
  - *I have many good qualities*
  - *Parts of me are OK*
  - *I'll like myself someday*
  - *God still loves me*
  - *My goldfish loves me*
  - *I am working on accepting myself*
  - *I am starting to feel more compassion for myself*

8.5 EFT for Cravings and Addictions

- The difference between cravings and addictions
- The role of anxiety in addictive behavior (Callahan)

Exercise 5: Chocolate Cravings

- Smell the chocolate – write down your SUD score for the craving!

- Tap for the substance itself, then for:
  - *Emotional associations with the substance*
  - *Events involving the substance*

© 2018 Energy Psychology Press

8.6 Aspects of Addiction

- The substance itself
- The feelings associated with the substance. Is it associated with celebration?
- What triggers the craving (events, times of day, people)
- Specific events occurring when the craving first started
- Losses: What did you used to have that you don't have now?
- Persistence – peel the onion, it may take years to identify all the aspects

© 2018 Energy Psychology Press

8.7 The Personal Peace Procedure

- Write down every negative event in a journal.
- SUD score for each one.
- There may be hundreds.
- Tap on one or two or three every day, till SUD is 0.

Tutorial #10: *"The Personal Peace Procedure"*

© 2018 Energy Psychology Press

8.8 Use Simple Techniques

8.8.1. Start with the simplest possible techniques. Simple methods like the Basic Recipe, the Full Basic Recipe, the Silent Movie Technique, and Tell the Story are often enough to produce change.

8.8.2. Other simple techniques are Talk and Tap and Rant and Tap. The client simply taps through all the points continuously, while talking or ranting about a problem.

TRAINER INSIGHTS

Question & Answer

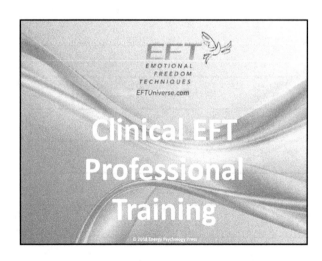

Clinical EFT Professional Training

Module 9

© 2018 Energy Psychology Press

Module 9 Learning Objectives

- **Participants will be able to:**
    1. Identify at least two of the conceptual frameworks within which EFT can be introduced to others.

Disclosure of Potential Conflicts of Interest: This workshop is designed to promote evidence-based practice and conform to current professional and ethical standards. While the trainer is receiving financial compensation, he or she is expected to avoid or minimize conflicts of interest, promote objective scientific and educational discourse, provide a fair and balanced assessment of therapeutic options, and present the curriculum free of commercial bias.

- Read *The EFT Manual* (3rd Ed) Chapter 3: The Basic Recipe, and Appendix A: The Full Basic Recipe

© 2018 Energy Psychology Press

9.1 Review of Foundational Concepts

- How do you prefer to introduce EFT?
- What is one sign of psychological reversal?
- Demonstrate the Full Basic Recipe and shortcut version.
- What is your favorite tapping point?
- Why does EFT focus on negative experiences instead of positive ones?

© 2018 Energy Psychology Press

Your Personal Experiences with EFT

9.2. What are some of the issues on which you have tried EFT?

- Cravings
- Phobias
- Allergies
- Intrusive memories
- Public speaking
- Insomnia
- Pain

© 2018 Energy Psychology Press

9.3 Other Foundational Concepts

- What's an example of a cognitive shift?
- Why are specific events important?
- Provide an example of an "aspect" of an event.
- What is the Generalization Effect?
- Why does EFT emphasize persistence?
- What's the first item you tap on when doing the Movie Technique?
- Describe the Personal Peace Procedure.
- Movie Technique Demo if time permits.

© 2018 Energy Psychology Press

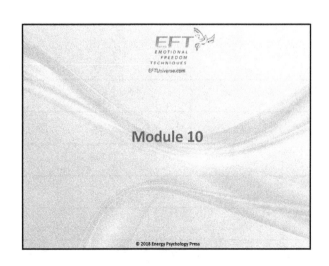

EFT
EMOTIONAL
FREEDOM
TECHNIQUES
EFTUniverse.com

Module 10

© 2018 Energy Psychology Press

Module 10 Learning Objectives

- **Participants will be able to:**

  1. Name at least one of EFT's *"Gentle Techniques."*
  2. Identify at least one clinical situation in which the Gentle Technique of *"Sneaking Up on the Problem"* is appropriate.

- Read *The EFT Manual* (3rd Ed) Chapter 6: The Gentle Techniques

© 2018 Energy Psychology Press

10. The Gentle Techniques

- Tearless Trauma
- Chasing the Pain
- Sneaking Up on the Problem

© 2018 Energy Psychology Press

10.1. Tearless Trauma

- If the SUD intensity of actually remembering is too high, don't remember, but guess.
- Keep the problem at arm's length.
- Keep it in a box, or play the movie behind a curtain.

© 2018 Energy Psychology Press

10.2 Dissociation in Tearless Trauma

- It is OK to dissociate.
  - o *Remember, dissociation serves a protective function for a child*
  - o *Tap on generalities to take the edge off*
- When the SUD score for the guess is 0-3, try actually remembering the event.
- Then proceed with EFT for specific events using the normal protocol.

10.3 Chasing the Pain

- Ask, "Where do you feel pain in your body?"
- Or, "Where do you feel the physical sensation of emotion in your body?"

10.3 Chasing the Pain (Continued)

- When the SUD goes down in that part, go to the next biggest SUD.
- An excellent gentle technique for clearing aspects of trauma without needing to talk about them or even identify them.

10.4 Physical Issues

- Look for the emotional causes of physical issues.
- Chasing the Pain can be used for any physical issue.
- Get very specific with physical description:

"Even though I have this sharp blue humming pain the size of a coin just below the center of my solar plexus..."

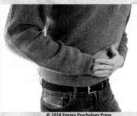

© 2018 Energy Psychology Press

10.5 When a Physical Symptom Persists

- Ask, "If there were an emotional issue behind this, what would it be?"
- If you don't know, guess.

© 2018 Energy Psychology Press

10.6 Sneaking Up - The Concept

- The technique to use for hopeless cognitions and core beliefs, the reasons why change is impossible.
- Reduces the intensity of a highly charged emotional memory.
- Bypasses rehearsed stories about "Why my life is this way."
- The coach neither agrees nor disagrees with the client, simply brackets the belief with "Even though" at the beginning and "I deeply and completely..." at the end.

© 2018 Energy Psychology Press

10.7 Sneaking Up - The Practice

- *10.8.* Start tapping immediately.
- *10.9.* Work the hopeless belief into a Setup Statement:
  - ○ *"Even though I can't tell anyone about this problem"*
  - ○ *"Even though years of therapy haven't helped"*
  - ○ *"Even though this problem is too big for me"*
  - ○ *"Even though I can't remember any specific events"*
  - ○ *"Even though it runs in my family"*
  - ○ *"Even though this disease is genetic"*
  - ○ *"Even though I can't recall any childhood events"*
  - ○ *"Even though I've had this problem my whole life"*

© 2018 Energy Psychology Press

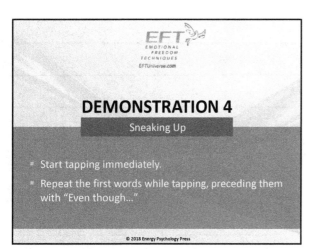

EFT
EMOTIONAL
FREEDOM
TECHNIQUES
EFTUniverse.com

DEMONSTRATION 4

Sneaking Up

- Start tapping immediately.
- Repeat the first words while tapping, preceding them with "Even though..."

© 2018 Energy Psychology Press

Exercises in Second Half of Professional Training

How exercises are different in the second half of Professional Training

- Up till now, the Trainer has been keeping time. From now on, for certain exercises, the trainer will give you a time frame and expect you to keep time when playing the role of coach.
- From now on, use the Session Notes forms to record your sessions.
- Use Sneaking Up and Sneaking Away regularly.
- Use the Full Basic Recipe including the 9 Gamut at least once in every exercise.
- When the Trainer walks around the room, ignore them. When in the Coach role, it's essential you be 100% present for your client.
- If you have questions, ask them at the beginning or the end of the exercise. Don't interrupt your session to talk to the Trainer or Emotional Assistants.

© 2018 Energy Psychology Press

Exercise 6: The Gentle Techniques Exercise

Pairs. One person in role of client, one coach

o **Client:** *Provide starting SUD. While tapping, speak about a habit you think you'll never get over, e.g., procrastination, interrupting, lateness, sense of direction, housecleaning. Pick the most hopeless cognitions, e.g., "I'll never get over this... My parents were this way... I'm doomed, it's my fate... I'll never be well..."*

o **Coach:** *Repeat the client's exact words. Start with "Even though..." in front, plus sometimes "I deeply and completely accept myself."*

o **Trainer** *won't provide a time frame. Will interrupt, after which coach uses Sneaking Away to terminate the session.*

© 2018 Energy Psychology Press

Exercise Feedback

What did you experience as a Coach?

Fill out Session Notes form.

What did you experience as a Client?

What did you experience as an Observer?

© 2018 Energy Psychology Press

EFT
EMOTIONAL
FREEDOM
TECHNIQUES
EFTUniverse.com

TRAINER INSIGHTS

Question & Answer

© 2018 Energy Psychology Press

EFT
EMOTIONAL
FREEDOM
TECHNIQUES
EFTUniverse.com

Module 11

© 2018 Energy Psychology Press

Module 11 Learning Objectives

▪ **Participants will be able to:**

1. List at least five cliches found in dysfunctional self-talk.

2. Identify at least two of the "four questions" used in style of Gesalt therapy known as "the work."

▪ Read *The EFT Manual* (3rd Ed) Chapter 7: Breaking the Habit of Being Yourself

© 2018 Energy Psychology Press

---

11. The Palace of Possibilities

11.1. You are born with infinite potential
▪ All doors in the Palace of Possibilities are open to us

11.2. Along the way, external voices tell us we can't do certain things
▪ These become "writings on our walls"

11.3. We stop going into these rooms
▪ We internalize those voices
▪ Eventually, we are living in a tiny space within the palace

© 2018 Energy Psychology Press

11.4 The Writings on Our Walls

- Family wisdom, authority figures
- We consult the writings on our walls when deciding what to do
- EFT is a good way to erase those old beliefs

© 2018 Energy Psychology Press

11.5 Clichés Are Writings on Our Walls

Examples of clichés we come to believe:
- Between a rock and a hard place.
- Better safe than sorry.
- The apple doesn't fall far from the tree.
- All the good men are taken.
- Money doesn't grow on trees.
- If you want something done right, do it yourself.
- Don't count your chickens before they're hatched.
- All good things come to an end.
- Expect the best; prepare for the worst.

© 2018 Energy Psychology Press

More Clichés

Examples of clichés we come to believe:
- I'm waiting for the other shoe to drop.
- Don't air your dirty laundry in public.
- Life's a bitch—and then you die.
- The only sure things are death and taxes.
- What makes you think you're so special?
- Don't make waves.
- The road to hell is paved with good intentions.
- Life sucks.
- It takes money to make money.

© 2018 Energy Psychology Press

More Clichés

Examples of clichés we come to believe:

- Too big for your britches.
- Curiosity killed the cat.
- What goes up, must come down.
- No pain, no gain.
- Don't come crying to me when...
- What will the neighbors say.
- The higher you rise, the harder you fall.
- No good deed goes unpunished.
- You can't make a silk purse out of a sow's ear.

© 2018 Energy Psychology Press

More Clichés

Examples of clichés we come to believe:

- Don't hold your breath.
- Quit while you're ahead.
- Misery loves company.
- You're over the hill.
- Spare the rod, spoil the child.
- Don't quit your day job.
- Nobody said it would be easy.
- The grass is always greener on the far side of the hill.
- Children should be seen, not heard.

© 2018 Energy Psychology Press

More Clichés

Examples of clichés we come to believe:

- Get off your high horse.
- The love of money is the root of all evil.
- Penny wise pound foolish.
- A fool and his money are soon parted.
- You can't buy love.
- Love hurts.
- Love is blind.
- You always hurt the one you love.
- I'll give you something to cry about.

© 2018 Energy Psychology Press

Your Self-Talk Reveals Your Clichés

11.6. We've become so accustomed to these clichés that we take them as given!

- We don't notice them
- We project them into the future

11.7. Listen to your self-talk

© 2018 Energy Psychology Press

Exercise 7: The Writings on Our Walls (Dyads)

- Use the Session Notes forms.
- Make a list of some of the clichés that are true for you.
- Write down "Belief SUD" for how true this is for you.
- Look for the underlying core beliefs.
- Consider specific incidents from your childhood that reinforced those beliefs.
- Find one incident. Write down new second SUD, "Incident SUD".
- Do EFT on specific incident until "Incident SUD" is low.
- Use the 9 Gamut at least once.
- What level is the Belief SUD now?
- Sneak away if the client's SUD is still high at the end of the session.

© 2018 Energy Psychology Press

Exercise Feedback

What did you experience as a Client?

What did you experience as a Coach?
Fill out Session Notes form.

© 2018 Energy Psychology Press

11.8 Ask yourself "The Four Questions" (Byron Katie)

- Is it true?
- Am I absolutely certain that it's true?
- How do I react, and what happens, when I believe that thought?
- Who would I be without that story?

© 2018 Energy Psychology Press

EFT Certified Practitioner-1 Requirements

- Online Course: The EFT Seminar, prerequisite to Professional Training. TheEFTSeminar.com
- EFT Professional Training class. 4 – 5 days.
- EFT-INT Online Test: This test covers EFT basics, such as those found in *The EFT Manual* and the Professional Training class.
- Proficiency Training: 2-day EFT Professional Practice Workshop. Demonstrating skills and proficiency 6 – 12 months later.
- Ethics Test: Based on two textbooks, *Ethics Handbook for Energy Healing Practitioners* and *Creating Healing Relationships*.

© 2018 Energy Psychology Press

EFT Certified Practitioner-1 Requirements

- Practical Application 1: Supervised delivery of 50 EFT sessions. Your notes from these sessions will be reviewed by a mentoring consultant. Your mentoring consultant is usually your EFT trainer.

- Forty-seven of your sessions are recorded on the Individual Session Notes form. Three are written up in detail using the case study guidelines form.

- Required readings, and 15 hours as client working your personal issues.

© 2018 Energy Psychology Press

EFT
EMOTIONAL
FREEDOM
TECHNIQUES
EFTUniverse.com

Module 12

© 2018 Energy Psychology Press

Module 12 Learning Objectives

- **Participants will be able to:**

1. Distinguish between a general issue and a specific event.
2. Identify at least one method of testing results other than providing Subjective Units of Distress.
3. Name at least one question used to identify a client's core beliefs.

- Read *The EFT Manual* (3rd Ed) Chapter 9: Professional Practice Techniques

© 2018 Energy Psychology Press

12. Tables and Legs

12.1. General issues are the table tops, e.g., procrastination, self-esteem, anxiety. Table tops are often core issues.

12.2. Specific events are the legs.
- You rarely make progress pounding the table.

12.3. With EFT we collapse one leg at a time.
- Eventually the whole table collapses.
- You don't always have to tap on every single leg.

© 2018 Energy Psychology Press

Tables and Legs Diagram

Table Top Issue: _____

Core Belief 1: _____ VOC Start: ___ VOC End ___
Core Belief 2: _____ VOC Start: ___ VOC End ___
Core Belief 3: _____ VOC Start: ___ VOC End ___

LEG #1
Event 1 Name
Age
Aspect 1:
SUD Start
SUD End
Aspect 2:
SUD Start
SUD End
Aspect 3:
SUD Start
SUD End
1

LEG #2
Event 2 Name
Age
Aspect 1:
SUD Start
SUD End
Aspect 2:
SUD Start
SUD End
Aspect X:
SUD Start
SUD End
2

LEG #3
Event 3 Name
Age
Aspect 1:
SUD Start
SUD End
Aspect 2:
SUD Start
SUD End
Aspect X:
SUD Start
SUD End
3

LEG #4
Event 4 Name
Age
Aspect 1:
SUD Start
SUD End
Aspect 2:
SUD Start
SUD End
Aspect 3:
SUD Start
SUD End
4

12.4 We Generalize from Early Experiences

- We recreate them, dragging the past into the present.
- Deep emotional learning reinforces the conditioned response of the neurological feedback loop.
- Creates new brain cells along those neural pathways.

12.5 Finding Core Issues

Ask questions:

- *Of which person in your past does this remind you?*
- *If you lived your life over, which event would you skip?*
- *What's the first time you ever experienced this feeling?*
- *If you were to guess at a deeper underlying emotion, what would it be?*

Write down three of your persistent Table Top issues.

12.6. Other Methods of Testing

Measuring SUD is not the only way of testing. Other methods include:

- Reenacting
- Asking pointed questions

If client is at 0:

- o *Have them vividly imagine sights, sounds, and smells*
- o *Have them try to get upset*

© 2018 Energy Psychology Press

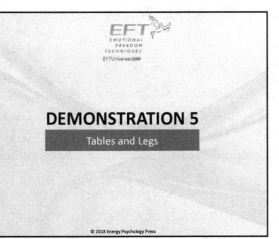

DEMONSTRATION 5
Tables and Legs

© 2018 Energy Psychology Press

Exercise 8: Tables and Legs (Dyads)

- As we've been working on this module, you've written down three of your own table top issues.
- When you're playing the role of coach, your job is to locate at least 5 legs in 7 minutes.
- Both coach and client tap continuously.
- Use the Tables and Legs diagram to write down the client's age and the name of each leg.
- Don't focus on tapping any of them down. Don't write down SUD, try and formulate Setups, or do any other part of EFT. The purpose of this exercise is simply to identify legs to tap on during future sessions. Make notes for future work.
- Sneak away if necessary.

© 2018 Energy Psychology Press

Tables, Legs, and Aspects Worksheet

Table Top Issue: _____

Core Belief 1: _____ VOC Start: ___ VOC End: ___

Core Belief 2: _____ VOC Start: ___ VOC End: ___

Core Belief 3: _____ VOC Start: ___ VOC End: ___

LEG #1
_____

Event 1 Name
_____

Age: _____
_____

Aspect 1:
_____

SUD Start: _____

SUD End: _____
_____

Aspect 2:
_____

SUD Start: _____

SUD End: _____
_____

Aspect 3:
_____

SUD Start: _____

SUD End: _____
_____

1

LEG #2
_____

Event 2 Name
_____

Age: _____
_____

Aspect 1:
_____

SUD Start: _____

SUD End: _____
_____

Aspect 2:
_____

SUD Start: _____

SUD End: _____
_____

Aspect 3:
_____

SUD Start: _____

SUD End: _____
_____

2

LEG #3
_____

Event 3 Name
_____

Age: _____
_____

Aspect 1:
_____

SUD Start: _____

SUD End: _____
_____

Aspect 2:
_____

SUD Start: _____

SUD End: _____
_____

Aspect 3:
_____

SUD Start: _____

SUD End: _____
_____

3

LEG #4
_____

Event 4 Name
_____

Age: _____
_____

Aspect 1:
_____

SUD Start: _____

SUD End: _____
_____

Aspect 2:
_____

SUD Start: _____

SUD End: _____
_____

Aspect 3:
_____

SUD Start: _____

SUD End: _____
_____

4

Exercise Feedback Slide

When you were playing the role of coach:
How many legs were you able to identify?

When you were playing the role of client:
Were there any surprises in the number or
intensity of the legs?

© 2018 Energy Psychology Press

EFT
EMOTIONAL
FREEDOM
TECHNIQUES
EFTUniverse.com

Module 13

© 2018 Energy Psychology Press

Module 13 Learning Objectives

- **Participants will be able to:**

  1. List at least 2 advantages of telephone or online sessions.

  2. Identify at least 2 essential prerequisites for such sessions.

- Read *The EFT Manual* (3rd Ed) Chapter 1: Inspiring Stories and Compelling Evidence

© 2018 Energy Psychology Press

13.1 EFT and Traditional Therapy or Coaching

- Therapy or coaching is usually a 1-hour session.
- EFT can be delivered the same way or:
  - On-demand phone sessions of 10 to 15 minutes
  - Intensives - 5 days, 1 day, a weekend
  - Via phone or video teleconferencing services like Facetime, Skype, Webinars, and Google Hangouts

© 2018 Energy Psychology Press

13.2 Considerations for Telephone Sessions

13.3. Client must know tapping points, because coach can't see whether or not client is tapping. Email the tapping diagram in advance. In advance, have them watch 9 Gamut video at 9Gamut.EFTuniverse.com.

13.4. Get SUD rating frequently, as you can't see visual stress cues like muscle tension, flushing, changes in breathing.

© 2018 Energy Psychology Press

13.5 Advantages of Telephone Sessions

Advantages of telephone sessions include:
- *Can be done at time of problem (e.g., during a panic attack, before a public speech, during a game)*
- *Eliminates drive time*
- *Can be done from home or an office*
- *May only need 5 minutes, reduced charges for client*
- *Expands service area of EFT practitioner*

© 2018 Energy Psychology Press

13.6 Considerations for Video Sessions

- Make sure the client has the appropriate software. Make sure it's up-to-date and you both have the latest version to minimize incompatibility issues. Schedule a tech test before the actual session.
- Look at the camera, not the video feedback screen on your computer. If possible, drag the video feedback screen close to the camera.
- Check your background. Make sure it looks professional. No laundry, personal photos, intrusive artwork, etc.

© 2018 Energy Psychology Press

13.6 Considerations for Video Sessions (Continued)

- Minimize distractions such as alerts, phone ringing, children, traffic, pets.
- Dress professionally.
- Make sure you have a high-speed internet connection. Be prepared for connectivity issues—flickery video, sound dropping. What is your refund policy for a tech failure? Can you offer sessions that you'll be doing from a hotel room?
- Switch to audio-only mode if video is consuming all available bandwidth.

© 2018 Energy Psychology Press

13.7 Phone or Video Sessions

- Double-check time zones.
- Record sessions if client wishes to replay them later.
- Use a headset to avoid neck and arm fatigue and to allow yourself to tap along.
- Listen intently.
- Use your intuition, but check it against the client's reality picture.

© 2018 Energy Psychology Press

DEMONSTRATION 6
Telephone Work

- Sit back to back to simulate a phone call.

- Walk through the tapping points while on the phone so the client knows when to switch.

- Feedback on exercise:
  - *What was the role of intuition?*

- Reality testing: Check intuitions against client's reality picture.

© 2018 Energy Psychology Press

Exercise 9: Telephone Work (Dyads)

- Use the Session Notes forms .
- Sit back to back to simulate a phone call.
- Coach: Walk through the tapping points while on the phone so the client knows when to switch.
- Client: Pick some upcoming event you're worried about, a presentation at work, a date, a doctor's visit, your mother-in-law coming to stay for a few days...
- Reality testing: Check intuitions against client's reality picture.
- Use the 9 Gamut at least once during the call.

© 2018 Energy Psychology Press

Exercise Feedback

What did you experience as a Coach?
What was the role of intuition?
Fill out Session Notes form.

What did you experience as a Client?

© 2018 Energy Psychology Press

Individual Session Notes for EFT Universe Certification

Please use this form to record session notes from each of the 47 client sessions required for certification.

EFT Candidate: _____   Session Date: _____

Client Initials: _____ Client Age: _____   Session # (1-47) _____

Mentoring Consultant: _____   Review Date: _____

Session # with client: Presenting Issue or Symptom:

Specific Recent Event:	
Aspect #1:	
	Beginning SUDS: (0-10) Ending SUDS: (0-10)
Aspect #2:	
	Beginning SUDS: (0-10) Ending SUDS: (0-10)

Childhood Event:	
Aspect #1:	
	Beginning SUDS: (0-10) Ending SUDS: (0-10)
Aspect #2:	
	Beginning SUDS: (0-10) Ending SUDS: (0-10)

Brief Narrative of Session (1-2 paragraphs):

EFT Techniques Used in This Session - 9 Gamut, Tearless Trauma, Sneaking Up, Chasing the Pain, Constricted Breathing, Movie Technique, Tell the Story, Reframing, Daisy Chaining, Tail Enders:

Testing Methods (other than SUDS) - Reenacting/Pointed Questions/Vivid Imagination/Actual Situation:

Most Difficult Challenge Arising in this Session:

Mentor Comments/Homework Assigned:

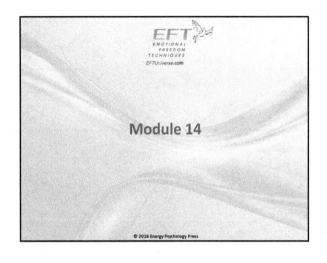

Module 14

© 2018 Energy Psychology Press

Module 14 Learning Objectives

▪ **Participants will be able to:**

1. Describe what is meant by the term "Validity of Cognition."

2. Describe how EFT's "tail-enders" method can identify a client's hidden objections to success.

3. Identify at least 2 ways in which life coaches must prepare to deal with psychological trauma.

▪ Read *The EFT Manual* (3rd Ed) Chapter 4: How People Use EFT for the Five Major Life Areas

© 2018 Energy Psychology Press

14.1 Tail-enders

Affirmations are powerful when they are in the present tense, vivid, and emotionally charged.

BUT they often come with tail-enders:

▪ *Affirmation: "I effortlessly maintain my ideal weight."*

Silent tail-ender: "…in your dreams."

▪ *Affirmation: "I live in abundance."*

Silent tail-ender: "…someday."

▪ *Affirmation: "My soul mate is with me now."*

Silent tail-ender: "…I wish."

▪ *Affirmation: "There is plenty of money."*

Silent tail-ender: "…for everyone else."

© 2018 Energy Psychology Press

14.2 Tail-enders (Continued)

- The true affirmation is the tail-ender.

- A tail-ender represents a tappable issue.

© 2018 Energy Psychology Press

14.3 Tail-enders (Continued)

Once we've dealt with the tail-ender, the affirmation isn't compromised by it.

- EFT is a tool for getting your affirmations to stick.
- Most "positive thinking" courses have you focus on the positive. EFT does not.
- Tapping away negative cognitions (clouds) allows positive ones (like the sky) to appear effortlessly.
- Bandaging a wound (concentrating on the positive) before cleaning it out (focusing on the negative) prevents real healing.

© 2018 Energy Psychology Press

14.4 VOC

- VOC - Validity of Cognition Scale
- How strongly you believe something:
  - ○ 0 – Don't believe at all
  - ○ 10 – Believe firmly

For the following exercise, score each statement below. How strong is your VOC?

Write down any especially powerful tail-enders next to the statement.

© 2018 Energy Psychology Press

14.5 Health/Body

- My body is vibrantly healthy

- I effortlessly maintain my ideal weight

- My body heals itself automatically and quickly

- My body is strong, fit, and flexible

- I have abundant energy

- I love the way I look

14.6 Wealth

- Money flows to me easily

- There is plenty for everyone

- My money is an expression of my spiritual values

- Unexpected money comes to me

- I love money and money loves me

- I live in abundance

14.7 Love

- Abundant love fills all my relationships

- I deserve huge amounts of love

- My perfect partner/soul mate is with me now

- I'm safe growing and changing while in a relationship

- Giving love is effortless for me

- Receiving love is effortless for me

14.8 Work

- My work is an expression of my creativity
- My work is in complete alignment with my life's mission
- I feel fulfilled by my work
- My work is filled with joy, ease, and light
- I throw myself enthusiastically into each day's work
- I have a glorious future ahead of me

© 2018 Energy Psychology Press

14.9 Spirit

- I am protected, loved, and guided by a Higher Power
- I fill my mind with nurturing ideas and positive thoughts
- I am a spiritual being on a human path
- My life effortlessly reflects my spiritual values
- My daily spiritual practice is strong
- I am one with a Higher Power

© 2018 Energy Psychology Press

Exercise 10: Tail-enders

Use the Session Notes forms.
When you're in the role of coach, ask:

- Where do you feel it in your body?
- What's your SUD Level?
- Tell me about the first incident in your life when you felt that physical feeling.
- Start tapping.

Coach: Use the 9 Gamut at least once during this session. Are you (a) making BIG circles (b) at the very EDGE of the client's peripheral vision?

© 2018 Energy Psychology Press

Exercise 11: Core Beliefs

Circle your most emotional tail enders.
Look for underlying core beliefs, such as:

- "I'm not good enough"
- "Life isn't fair"
- "My needs don't matter"

Give each one a VOC score.
Find specific childhood events that reinforced those beliefs.
Find one particular incident and write down the SUD score.
Tap on event till SUD is low. Use 9 Gamut at least once.
Measure VOC again after tapping on event.
Sneak away if client's SUD is still high at end of session.
Use the Session Notes form throughout.

© 2018 Energy Psychology Press

Exercise Feedback

When you played the role of coach, what did you learn? What was easiest? Most challenging?

What was your experience filling out the Session Notes form?

When you played the role of client, were there any surprises?

© 2018 Energy Psychology Press

14.10 When Old Self-Concepts Collapse

It is sometimes necessary to introduce positive self-concepts.

- Occasionally with EFT, old negative self-concepts collapse completely and unexpectedly in the course of a session. This creates a void, leaving the client feeling disoriented.
- Be ready to introduce positive self-concepts.
- Use the goals stated by client on their intake form.

positive
negative

© 2018 Energy Psychology Press

Individual Session Notes for EFT Universe Certification

Please use this form to record session notes from each of the 47 client sessions required for certification.

EFT Candidate: _____   Session Date: _____

Client Initials: _____   Client Age: _____   Session # (1-47) _____

Mentoring Consultant: _____   Review Date: _____

Session # with client: Presenting Issue or Symptom:

Specific Recent Event:		
Aspect #1:		
	Beginning SUDS: (0-10)	Ending SUDS: (0-10)
Aspect #2:		
	Beginning SUDS: (0-10)	Ending SUDS: (0-10)

Childhood Event:		
Aspect #1:		
	Beginning SUDS: (0-10)	Ending SUDS: (0-10)
Aspect #2:		
	Beginning SUDS: (0-10)	Ending SUDS: (0-10)

Brief Narrative of Session (1-2 paragraphs):

EFT Techniques Used in This Session - 9 Gamut, Tearless Trauma, Sneaking Up, Chasing the Pain, Constricted Breathing, Movie Technique, Tell the Story, Reframing, Daisy Chaining, Tail Enders:

Testing Methods (other than SUDS) - Reenacting/Pointed Questions/Vivid Imagination/Actual Situation:

Most Difficult Challenge Arising in this Session:

Mentor Comments/Homework Assigned:

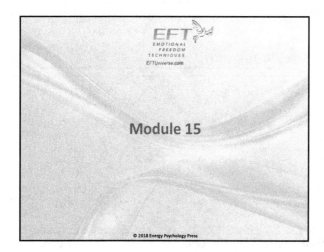

Module 15 Learning Objectives

- **Participants will be able to:**

  1. Name two symptoms of psychological trauma.

  2. Identify one of the necessary conditions for memory reconsolidation and extinction.

- Read *Psychological Trauma: Healing Its Roots in Body, Brain and Memory*

15. Psychological Trauma

15.1. Psychological trauma is widespread.

- One in 10 boys is molested, and one in five girls, usually by a family member.
- Sixty percent of older children witness or experience victimization in a given year. Close to half experience physical assault, and 25% witness domestic or community violence.
- Women are twice as likely to be victims of domestic violence than they are to get breast cancer.
- During the period of the wars in Iraq and Afghanistan, more Americans died at the hands of family members than were killed in the Middle East.

(Gorey & Leslie, 1997; U.S. Department of Health and Human Services, 2012; van der Kolk, 2014)

© 2018 Energy Psychology Press

© 2018 Energy Psychology Press

15.2 Unexpected Encounters with Trauma

- EFT coaches often encounter trauma unexpectedly in clients. Examples include:
  - A client books a series of sessions for overcoming money obstacles, and during the second session he has a flashback to childhood molestation by a baby-sitter.
  - A client who says she recalls "no childhood memories" recovers a terrifying memory fragment of abuse while tapping on an unrelated issue.
  - A client states that she had a "happy childhood," yet the coach has an intuitive sense that abuse lies below the surface.
  - Despite having strong conscious motivation to change, a client makes no progress on a long-term issue such as obesity.
  - Without warning, in the middle of a session, a client's body begins to shake violently as he processes an intense emotion.

© 2018 Energy Psychology Press

15.3 Preparation for Trauma

- For this reason, EFT coaches need to be prepared to deal with trauma. Strategies include:
  - ○ *Being familiar with the signs and symptoms of trauma, such as flashbacks, nightmares, and intrusive thoughts.*
  - ○ *Having the ability to distinguish genuine trauma from transient psychological distress.*
  - ○ *Maintaining a list of local licensed mental health professionals trained in trauma to whom clients can be referred.*
  - ○ *Educating yourself about trauma by reading books, attending workshops such as the EFT Universe specialty workshops, and using online resources such as the Psychological Trauma course.*

© 2018 Energy Psychology Press

15.3 Preparation for Trauma (Continued)

- ○ *Having written procedures for dealing with unexpected trauma.*
- ○ *Discussing the possibility of traumatic recall with clients at appropriate intervals.*
- ○ *Being alert to the possibility of retraumatization.*
- ○ *Seeking supervision when you are uncertain as to whether a case lies within your scope of practice.*

© 2018 Energy Psychology Press

15.4 EFT Techniques for Trauma

- Common EFT procedures for dealing with trauma
  - ○ *Keep tapping. Don't stop the session, get so drawn into the client's story that you forget to tap, or otherwise abandon the client.*
  - ○ *Maintain eye contact and emotional presence. Traumatized clients may re-experience emotions intensely, and the practitioner's presence may feel like a lifeline to the client.*
  - ○ *Perform the 9 Gamut technique repeatedly, using slow eye movements and general statements.*
  - ○ *Notice your own triggering. Intense emotions in the client often trigger the coach, and your responsibility is to set your reactions aside for future processing, so that you can be fully present for your client.*

© 2018 Energy Psychology Press

15.4 EFT Techniques for Trauma (Continued)

- More EFT procedures for dealing with trauma:
  - *Resourcing. Reminding the client of positive elements of their lives. Trauma can overwhelm a client and positive statements may help install a counterbalancing narrative.*
  - *Using general Setup Statements instead of focusing on specific events.*
  - *Reframing. Placing a neutral or positive frame around negative events to remind the client of safety, the present, and their current-life resources.*
  - *Orienting the client to the present moment. Traumatized clients often reexperience the past as though it were the present.*

© 2018 Energy Psychology Press

15.5 Memory Reconsolidation and Extinction

- The limbic midbrain, responsible for learning, memory, and emotion, is the fastest-growing brain region for the first 18 months of life.
- Emotional memories, especially those formed early in life before the development of language, are neurological rather than cognitive, locked into long-term memory.
  - *For example, a neglected infant might develop a worldview that "my needs don't matter" at the level of neurons in the hippocampus, much more basic than a core belief stored in the cerebrum at a later stage of cognitive development.*

© 2018 Energy Psychology Press

15.5 Memory Reconsolidation and Extinction (Continued)

- These "emotional learnings" were long thought to be permanent, "locked into the brain by extraordinary durable synapses." Early-life trauma is notoriously difficult to remedy.
- Recent research shows that, under certain conditions, emotional learnings become "labile" and susceptible to revision.
- The "reconsolidation window" lasts for about 4 hours after reactivation of the memory or experience.

© 2018 Energy Psychology Press

15.6 The "Transformation Sequence"

- The are three conditions necessary for memory reconsolidation:
  - ○ *Vivid reexposure to the memory or experience must occur.*
  - ○ *At the same time, a contradictory experience or memory ("juxtaposition experience") must be activated.*
  - ○ *Several repetitions of the juxtaposition experience may be necessary in order for the new worldview to overwrite the old one.*

(Ecker, Ticic, & Hulley, 2012)

15.7 How EFT Incorporates the Three Steps

- *Vivid Reexposure:* The first part of the Setup Statement: "Even though (the problem)..."
- *Juxtaposition Experience:* (a) Somatic soothing in the form of tapping, (b) brain stimulation via the 9 Gamut, and (c) the neutral cognitive frame provided by the second part of the Setup: "...I deeply and completely accept myself."
- *Repetition:* (a) Testing using SUD, (b) repeated rounds of tapping till SUD is 0, and (c) identifying and tapping on all Aspects encoded in the Trauma Capsule.

EFT
EMOTIONAL
FREEDOM
TECHNIQUES
EFTUniverse.com

TRAINER INSIGHTS

Question & Answer

Module 16

© 2018 Energy Psychology Press

Module 16 Learning Objectives

- **Participants will be able to:**

   1. Describe one recommended change to EFT's Basic Recipe when working with preteen children.

   2. Define "transference."

   3. Define "projection."

- Read *The EFT Manual* (3rd Ed) Chapters 9 and 10:
    Professional Practice Techniques
    Confronting Massive Human Suffering

© 2018 Energy Psychology Press

16.1 Using EFT with Children

- Young children love EFT.
- Focus on facts, rather than feelings.
- Pay rigorous attention to exact words.
    - *They make sense to the child, though they may not make sense to you.*
- Often, the child will respond immediately.
- Keep the language very simple.
    - *Just "I'm OK" or "I'm a good kid" in the Setup Statement.*
- Tappy Bear, drawings, and other ways of evoking the imagination of the child can be useful.

© 2018 Energy Psychology Press

16.2 Using EFT with Children (Continued)

Use age-appropriate strategies

- For babies, the parent can tap on the child or on themselves
- Teenagers can tap on themselves
- Tap along with YouTube videos

© 2018 Energy Psychology Press

© 2018 Energy Psychology Press

16.3 Delivering EFT in Groups

- Each person picks their own issue.
- Leader can tap generally for everyone, or ask for a demonstration subject and tap with them while the rest of the group borrows benefits.
- Leader uses general Setup Statements that represent problems common to universal human experience, such as: "Even though…" followed by generalities such as: "…I was abandoned… the bad experience … it shouldn't have happened…"
- Participants focus on their own issue while they watch someone else's session. Each person assesses their own SUD level before and after tapping.
- Choose participant problems that are amenable to change in a limited time frame of 5-15 minutes. Avoid traumas such as assault, abuse, and any issue more appropriate to private sessions.

© 2018 Energy Psychology Press

16.3 Delivering EFT in Groups (Continued)

- If you're the leader, use EFT on some easy target first, like the toe touching exercise.
- Doing Demonstrations:
  - *Ask for participant problems, pick an easy one.*
  - *Use the Gentle Techniques if participant isn't able to talk about the problem.*
  - *How to deal with difficult participants.*
- For an ongoing group, determine if potential member is suitable (intake form or interview).

© 2018 Energy Psychology Press

16.4 Scope of Practice

EFT is usually defined as peer-to-peer coaching, not therapy.

- Strictly: No diagnosis or treatment. No medical or psychological advice.
- If you are a licensed mental health provider, you can use EFT within your practice.
- The focus is on teaching a self-help tool to the client.
- Avoid dependency, transference, countertransference.

© 2018 Energy Psychology Press

16.5 Transference and Countertransference

- *Transference:* Feelings
(e.g., parental affection, transferred by client onto coach)

- *Countertransference:* Projected by coach onto client
(e.g., need to be liked)

© 2018 Energy Psychology Press

16.6 Scope of Practice

- Informed Consent

- Forms for Practitioners

- Ethics Code on website

16.7 Be Aware of Ethical Issues

Examples from *Ethics Handbook for Energy Healing Practitioners*:

- Wife starts sessions, refers her husband, and you discover infidelity
- Colleague who sends inflammatory emails
- Two clients who are both dog lovers and single
- Using the work of others without attribution

16.8 Nine Differences Between Coaching & Psychotherapy

1. Psychotherapy can provide *diagnosis* using the DSM (Diagnostic & Statistical Manual). A primary focus of psychotherapy is the identification and diagnosis of mental disorders. Coaching *does not diagnose*.

2. Psychotherapy can provide diagnosis *independent* of the client's self-assessment. This function is recognized by third parties such as the courts. Coaching, by way of contrast, relies on the client's *self-assessment*.

3. Psychotherapy can use diagnoses to *treat clinical disorders* like anxiety and depression. Coaching does not treat, claim that it is treatment, or use the word *treatment*.

16.8 Nine Differences Between Coaching & Psychotherapy (Continued)

4. The types of goals are different. Psychotherapy goals typically involve *treatment of a mental disorder* by the therapist. Coaching goals typically focus on *quality of life*.

5. Who sets goals is different. In psychotherapy they may be set by the therapist after diagnosis. Goals in coaching are typically *self-identified by the client*.

16.8 Nine Differences Between Coaching & Psychotherapy (Continued)

6. Psychotherapy typically involves recognized *power differentials* between client and therapists. This vulnerability of clients gives psychotherapists legal and ethical responsibilities. Coaching is in the nature of a *supportive peer-to-peer relationship*, with the results evaluated by the client, and is designed to avoid these power differentials.

7. The focus of much psychotherapy is *intervention by the therapist*. The focus of much coaching is the *teaching of self-help tools*.

16.8 Nine Differences Between Coaching & Psychotherapy (Continued)

8. Psychotherapy may be provided by *primary caregivers* such as hospitals. Coaching is rarely associated with primary care.

9. Coaches are required to *refer* clients to psychotherapists or psychiatrists if the client's problem is outside their scope of practice. Psychotherapists are those *to whom* clients are referred.

Using the Full Range of Techniques

Demo (7) or Exercise (12).

© 2018 Energy Psychology Press

Help Healing. Help EFT. Get Involved!

Volunteering for EFT Humanitarian Work:
Volunteer.EFTuniverse.com
Start a Tapping Circle, Online or in Person:
TappingCircles.EFTuniverse.com
Volunteer for the Veterans Stress Project:
www.StressProject.org
Donate to Research:
www.NIIH.org
Get Informed about Research:
Research.EFTuniverse.com
*Add a Link for a Free Download of the **Mini Manual** on Your Web Site:*
www.TappingGift.com

© 2018 Energy Psychology Press

Individual Session Notes for EFT Universe Certification

Please use this form to record session notes from each of the 47 client sessions required for certification.

EFT Candidate: _____   Session Date: _____

Client Initials: _____ Client Age: _____   Session # (1-47) _____

Mentoring Consultant: _____   Review Date: _____

Session # with client: Presenting Issue or Symptom:

Specific Recent Event:	
Aspect #1:	
	Beginning SUDS: (0-10) Ending SUDS: (0-10)
Aspect #2:	
	Beginning SUDS: (0-10) Ending SUDS: (0-10)

Childhood Event:	
Aspect #1:	
	Beginning SUDS: (0-10) Ending SUDS: (0-10)
Aspect #2:	
	Beginning SUDS: (0-10) Ending SUDS: (0-10)

Brief Narrative of Session (1-2 paragraphs):

EFT Techniques Used in This Session - 9 Gamut, Tearless Trauma, Sneaking Up, Chasing the Pain, Constricted Breathing, Movie Technique, Tell the Story, Reframing, Daisy Chaining, Tail Enders:

Testing Methods (other than SUDS) - Reenacting/Pointed Questions/Vivid Imagination/Actual Situation:

Most Difficult Challenge Arising in this Session:

Mentor Comments/Homework Assigned:

Individual Session Notes for EFT Universe Certification

Please use this form to record session notes from each of the 47 client sessions required for certification.

EFT Candidate: _____   Session Date: _____

Client Initials: _____ Client Age: _____   Session # (1-47) _____

Mentoring Consultant: _____   Review Date: _____

Session # with client: Presenting Issue or Symptom:

Specific Recent Event:	
Aspect #1:	
	Beginning SUDS: (0-10) Ending SUDS: (0-10)
Aspect #2:	
	Beginning SUDS: (0-10) Ending SUDS: (0-10)

Childhood Event:	
Aspect #1:	
	Beginning SUDS: (0-10) Ending SUDS: (0-10)
Aspect #2:	
	Beginning SUDS: (0-10) Ending SUDS: (0-10)

Brief Narrative of Session (1-2 paragraphs):

EFT Techniques Used in This Session - 9 Gamut, Tearless Trauma, Sneaking Up, Chasing the Pain, Constricted Breathing, Movie Technique, Tell the Story, Reframing, Daisy Chaining, Tail Enders:

Testing Methods (other than SUDS) - Reenacting/Pointed Questions/Vivid Imagination/Actual Situation:

Most Difficult Challenge Arising in this Session:

Mentor Comments/Homework Assigned:

CPSIA information can be obtained
at www.ICGtesting.com
Printed in the USA
BVHW011951200619

551556BV00010B/195/P